ART IN EVERY DAY

ART IN EVERY DAY

VOLUME II

SASH KALANSURIYA

PALMETTO
PUBLISHING
Charleston, SC
www.PalmettoPublishing.com

Art In Every Day

First Edition

Paperback ISBN: 979-8-8229-0818-5

POEMS

To examine life we look at everything;

Gladness and Pain.

ENDURANCE

Boxwood

You remember the days at Boxwood
Almost like a dream
And yet that likeness of home,
Perfect as it seems,
Was nothing more than
The sum of our hearts.

We would grow to be men
And yet we had no plan but freedom
Living daily, playing as if we had
Nothing else to do
Nowhere else to be.
So it seems those things would play
Upon our minds later,
When we were at the limit
Of what a man can take,
And so we broke into laughter
That brought us tears.

The less of everything
Was all you could call for
When you needed help
And no one was there.
Peace falls like that
Let it come.

Many Happy Returns

With a new year
Comes many expectations.
A hope you'll meet someone
And fall in love
Like you never had before.
The right one.
The job you always wanted
But never seemed to get.
Things will work out this year
Or so you say
Because you never really know.

Life twists and turns
Like the stalk you hold
From the daisy you found
Early in the day.
There is a lightness
That wakes you
Delicate as love can be.
Who will be the girl
What color will her eyes be
Brown or blue?
How will she sound when she speaks?
It matters to you

When you finally decide
Because not-knowing
Can be like torture.

For the new year
We raise a toast
For all the year can bring
Health
Success.
We will grow older but stronger
And remember what our parents told for
All they know is wisdom.
May we be kind
And love each other
Give back all we're blessed with
For all of that
And Many Happy Returns!

First Scene

Growing up we always had each other
Someone to sit beside and play with.
He held me tight so I wouldn't fall
And placed me on his lap when I was born
And when he held me there was an unmistakable joy.
You could see it in every picture
There was gentleness and peace
And good will, we were brothers.
Though you could tell us apart
We were one and the same.
If anyone would keep me from harm
I knew he would do that.
We never fought and he never went against me
No matter what.
That was the way we always were.
I wore his old clothes and rode his old bike
We liked all the same things and ate together.
When you grow up with someone
They're a part of you and there's nothing like that.
He was there at every scene
Loyal as anyone could be.
I can't imagine going on without him
We're too close for that.
It wouldn't be the same.

Able

Sitting in a coffee shop
One can think of a thousand different things
Not to do.
A relationship not to approach
A stranger not to meet.
When you live inside yourself
The child who needs help
Is no more a child
Than you are.
Living alone has its comfort
But also its sorrow.
How do you climb out
To find your able.
You are as much a part of the world
As they are.
Together they make you whole.
Every life is as much a part of you
As you are them.
Whatever voice you hear
Is someone calling you
To say you are as much needed
As they are.
You are not alone.
More than that,
You are able.
Just believe you are.

And So Love Goes

A man can only take so much
Till he falls like a child
Because sometimes more is more
And less is less.

Until we figure out these things
We can only guess
What the words will be
And what we allow them.

Hush the night call the sun
Wait for her to come.
Let her take her time
Because you know it's worth it.

So you're left to wait
Waiting to discover
What her kind eyes will tell you
Without a breath.

Is it love you wonder
What you're feeling
Or is it something more
Something more like faith or God or grace?

All the holy things
You could never live without
Sometimes bad things
Come to good people too.

Go on and hope for the best
For all we have is blessed
And let us burn brighter
Like the stars.

The Bride Not Content

Not every marriage is happy
Not every one starts that way.
We have so many ideas
Of what we want.
It doesn't always come true.
So do we look disappointed
And scream and fight
Or do we find a way to find peace?

Some weddings start off happy
And fall apart.
It's human nature to always want more.
To be dissatisfied
To feel restless and wanting someone new.
So how do we stay as one?
We hear each other
We sacrifice and pay dues.
What else could we do?

To fall in love is a promise
To stay together for better or worse
Good and bad.
We stay together in sickness and health
And there's beauty in that.

Love is something we build
One day we look back
Our heart warms at what we had.

Love is a union
We stay till we're old and grey.
We settle in some ways
And yet there's much to gain
By trying and pushing each other
To see the best in all of us
See the good in everything
Every trial, every shortcoming,
Every failure.
Love builds that way.

Reality Sets In

There's a moment when you're young
And you realize you can't go on the same way.
You need to grow up and take care of things.
Honor thy mother and father
And build a future.

You must depend on yourself.
You really aren't that young anymore
And you can see it on your face in the mirror
That the time is passing.

It's time to find someone to be with
So you will not be alone
For solitude has a time and place, and love another.
If you miss her now you might not see her again.

Live without regret, take pride in what you do.
One day you will look back at what you did and smile
If you were kind and good, decent, and true.
How you judge is based on what you know
So read greatly, you may benefit the world.

Clarify

When you say a word
You don't have to mean it.
Words are words
Until you say them
No one really cares.
It's wise to be careful
But so many words are said
That you can say it back
If you had a mouth like mine
Sorry would be the first word you learned.
So someone asks to clarify
You never say what you really said
Or you'll be saying sorry a lot
And forget what you meant to say
It's easy to lose track
Of what you thought and what you said
So maybe say everything you want
The first time you say it
Just be ready
To duck when they swing
Or runaway somewhere
And stay low for a while.

Every Good Boy Does Fine

Every lesson you ever learned
There was a price to pay
Some exchange of time or pain
To soak in.

There is a measure for days
And the collective wisdom
We are earning
Just by sitting still and listening.

Soon that energy will grow
Too fast to wait
And we must stand up and live
And take for school what we see.

Somewhere between books,
The world about,
To which we apply what we know
We find insight.

For we have tapped the rock
To see the diamond within
By seeing men and going places
And taking note and seeing why
Where others can only accept.

There is danger
In going your own way
But it never stopped great men
From going.

Hear every side
Gain experience by doing
Lower your pride
And submit to the willingness to learn.

Little by little
Small pieces add up a lot
And you will not know
What you become
Because you were never really counting.

Lift your head
And hear the voices praising you.

Anticipation

What is the point of waiting
When you're nearing halfway
And your life hasn't begun?
You've spent your life learning
And there's no one to share with.
The work is the reward
But you still need love.
You're only human.
The longer you wait
The more you feel resigned to love
And not embracing.
That is not what love should be.
It should be like racing to meet
The only person who ever made you feel this way.
To be complete.

So

In a watchful sun
The world's turning
Every bit of technology
Is keeping track too.
Everywhere you go
People are watching
Their eyes are over you.
The patterns of your breathing
They are studying.

Is it any wonder
You feel discomfort
And so much anger
At what they do?
To protect you
You must sacrifice
But the price is too high
When any hope
Of privacy is taken
And the joy of living is lost.

What hell is this
To be always restrained
Even in your thinking
The words you want to say
You will not say them.
They will collect it as evidence
And prove you're guilty
For being you.
They will make you feel shame.
Isolation is what you get.
Only wasted time.

Nowhere To Go

I feel like I'm trapped
And there's no where to get out
And there's nowhere to go.
Life is just one long never-ending thing.

When we were young
It was so much different.
I was happier then
And still I was going nowhere.

Maybe you can't go nowhere forever
As hard as you try
You'll end up somewhere
Even for a little while.

Maybe that somewhere
Is where you're supposed to be.
Whether you were early or late
Whether you're there or not.

Everyone's going somewhere
You'll get there too.
Even when you least expect it.

Tea Party

There's nothing like a warm drink
To warm your soul
For us to sit and talk about the things we want.
I never shared my heart with anyone
Not the way I look forward to you.

Some days I drink alone
And I'm waiting for someone to join me.
Everyone wants the same things in life
To be proud of the life they built
To be happy and secure that the future will be good.

The hardest part is the fear of losing
And comparing yourself and feeling small.
It doesn't really matter what they say
If you say 'I like who I am.'
'I'm proud of where I am right now
There's nothing else I need.'

When you remind yourself
Of where you've been, and where you'll go,
And see completion,
In all you've earned along the way,
You will not ask for any more
And so much will be there.

A New Car

I never cared for materials things
But I remember the first car I bought.
How we went shopping together
Me and mom.
I just got a new job
After graduating
I needed a way to get there.
I wasn't that excited
It was really a necessary thing.
The car was black
With a black interior
It was called The Batmobile
It was just the way my brother wanted.
Now that car's a part of me
Something in my life
I've taken far and wide
Driving down to Florida
With mom and dad
Interviews and parties
And living alone.
It's been with me through everything
I wonder what kind of car
I'll get the next time
Maybe a white one
This one still has miles to go

Many roads to see.
Somedays when I'm driving
I don't know where I'm going
But I feel lucky to be free.

Tom Cruise

A million dollar smile can take you far
But how much further the drive to work hard
And live clean.
An honesty and sensibility
To carry yourself with grace.
There is a still a place for justice
For those who judge well
And live in wisdom.
Even when we fall
We are true to what we say.
To have stardom is to expose yourself
To so much jealousy and ridicule
And the gossip of men will never cease.
When you are good
All those things will fade
And your memory live
And your smile remain.
You have stood through all
And you deserve your success
Your fame your glory
For you have shown yourself
Among the best of men
For those who love you will always do.

Last Page

Humble yourself the greater you are
That's what the elders say.
Lead them from behind
So you will not burden.
There is wisdom in that.
Wise men from many nations
Have gathered
To build the world the right way.
There is no vanity in peace.
Make no presumption
We become what we think
Big words mean little
So say what you mean when you say it.
When you're busy doing
You don't have time to dwell.
You're busy doing the things
That earn you praise.
So we build the world this way.
When we listen
Good things will come.
If we are patient
We learn to wait.

REBIRTH

Walking Without

I thought I'd take a walk one day
And leave behind the things I usually take.
The things I was hoping for
Everything I regretted doing.
An absence of mind
I may indulge in.
Walking far away from everyone
As if I came to be just now.
One thought at a time
One self, this kingdom, one peace.
And when the wind blows it makes no sound
It makes no difference to me.
How far will I go before I tire?
How long will I go before I rest?
Until I collapse or until
I cease to find the meaning
Of 'being', and being alone.

Things Without A Name

I wish I understood
What the purpose was
For all this suffering.
What does it mean to be different
To see the truth
As clear as one
Can shake a hand
And feel the whole
Weight of a person?

If I could see something
I would say something
But I can only feel
What it is inside.

All That Waits For No One

There's no real shelter
That love offers
Greater than your mother and father.
You may fall in love
And start a new life
But you'll never depend on them the same
And you'll never have peace like childhood
And they were there from the first day
Taking you and guiding you.
The ones to fall back on
When the world's against you
There's no peace like childhood
No love like theirs
If you search for something greater
It simply won't be found.

Love Always Seems That Way

When you're used to getting
Everything you want
It's kind of hard when you don't
Turn things over in your mind
Try to see a reason why.
Sometimes there is no reason
It's just the way it goes.
Sometimes we fail in love
As anything else
Never connecting
With those we desire.
You're ready to give up.
It's not worth the time
Like every imperfection
Or any flaw
Facing all to see.

There are days it's really not you it's them
Though you've heard it before
It's hard to justify.
Every sign you saw was untrue
And you let it seem
More than it was due.
The mind plays tricks like that.
You oughta be careful.

You could believe anything
If you spent long enough
And gave no time to breath.
You have a cross for these things
Idols of holy value,
For times when things turn out
Not the way you pictured.
There's no way to stop
When the dreadful thing is done.
It's right that love goes bad.
Some things never end
A record
Plays over
Your last nerve
Falls apart.

The Dislocated Shoulder

The separation of the body and the mind.
Who we are and what we appear.
How do we feel inside?
Vital organs go unnoticed
Till something goes awry.
All the separate parts
Make up the whole
And every one counts for something
Why is it pain
That makes us recall
Something we never cared about?

A dislocated shoulder
Is far away from the mind
And yet it matters
For the mind feels all.
The mind will comfort
And the mind will tear
Just like a shoulder
Out of place for a time.
If we place the shoulder
The mind will heal too.
If not they both suffer.
They are two but they are connected.

So the country that stands apart
Is still one that works together
With the greater whole.
But only through conflict do we understand
The demands of the other
For else they go unnoticed.
The central mind controls all
But seldom does it feel
Until something is broken
Or separated or acting out in some way.
Then it takes the mind to heal
What the body would suffer otherwise.
And the mind to think what should be done.
But who has all that power?
And what exactly should we do?

Life Is What You Make It

I.

What creation that comes from the mind
Matters like this one.
The vast creation of living
All we experience and what we are
Through every sense we allow.
The life we build though love and laughter.
The stories we share and the memories between us.
They stay deep inside.
Where do we go?

II.

There is no reception
Without vision and feeling
Like circuits of the electric board
We switch on to fire
All we imagine is levitating
There is no way to touch it
Unless we are present.
That is the gift of being
Blurring with fantasy
There is a place for that
For we are human
We need control.

Are we satisfied
With what we do
Or is it just a game
Living and dying?
Is there an answer as to why?
I will keep searching
Because I want to know
And I know it's out there.
I have all my life to see.

Who Will Marry Our Daughters?

When you raise a child
You demand a lot
From them and from you.
When it's a daughter
How great the fear
Where you place her
And the name she's given.
You pray she will be safe
And provided for
When she marries one day.
You teach her
How to be strong and always grateful
To be kind and cheerful
To have faith.
The more she remains alone
The more you dread
She will stay that way.
You worry sick
That everything you
planned
Was for naught.
It's an investment
You pray
your heart is given
some return.

That is when you take control
Of your own fate
Push her
To never settle.
She will cultivate herself
Show a man how to be.
She will know peace
And see harmony
In what she made.

A Wealth of Ideas

There is a wealth of ideas
Swimming in your brain
Waiting for you to bring them out
And share them.

If you are silent
No one will know
And you will go unnoticed
And unappreciated.

When it is time
Stand up and speak
Or sit down and write
See what you have inside.

Do not think
It is not important
What you have to say
Every word matters
From what we learn.

That is how we grow.

Point Pleasant

In the cold of winter
You remember Point Pleasant
The beaches and the women
The warmth of the sun
Your feet playing in the sand
Looking for cover.
How good it feels to feel this way
Walking by the sea
Letting the water run over your feet
How many elements you feel at one time
How brave the children to face the sea
They know no fear
They are too young to be afraid
They are too happy to wait
For they are free.
They cast a shadow greater than me
I feel no shame, only joy.
This is what it means
To ask for nothing.

Was It Someone You Loved?

Everyone has worries.
Some never go away.
New ones arise
Every other day.
A fear of death
Of never amounting
To anything.

What good will they do
Unless you face them?
Realize they're there
And take action
Say if I run I will feel better.
If I breathe I will stop this thought
If I'm useless I will find use.

Enter your mind and seek to understand.
What are you able to do?
How do you stop this?
You can write it out
You can talk it through
But please do something.

Find the time to laugh
To connect, to be still.
Find faith in the good, the strong, the brave, and
Let your fears fall away.

So many thoughts
To be defined that way.
Where you doubt yourself
You will see comfort
Helping those along
More in need than
Even you.

To Laugh Again

Dear friend
How good it feels
To laugh again.
So isolated
I have been
And now I see again
A reason to live
To feel joy
Like riding a bike
For the first time
Or hearing your favorite song
Playing on the radio.
How good it feels
To laugh again.
'So warm' she says
'How much warmer
For years without.'

The Builder

To lift weights is a type of freedom
How far are you willing to go?
Will you stop at 10
Or will you do more?
The further you push yourself
The stronger you become.

Everyone starts from somewhere
It's a lesson in perseverance.
The more you dedicate the time
And the more energy you spend
The more growth you see.
A steady gain from what you do.

It's the principal that shows
The harder you work the more you get
Through personal industry
You will build the drive
To win the great
And show the world you
Built yourself.

Recommendation Letter

To say something for you
Would be too difficult
For I know no one better
And it's hard to express
In words how it feels
To have your affection
And support.
You have always been there
When everyone else was gone
And you never did anything unkind to me.
How could that be?

To laugh along with you
And be near
Is as close to love as I have felt
When we're together we are better
For we know each other so well
We do not have to speak
And our laughter adds upon the other
For we have known peace
For so long
And it will never falter
If we stay this way.

There is no heart as good as yours
Everything we've been through
Is everything to me.
You will never be replaced
You will always be your own person,
And I love you for that.

Freestyle

See the ghost that plays in you.
What rhythm are you inviting?
Somewhere in the keys
You will start to open.
In the rainy season
When the weather blows white
The searchlights will be out
And you will be terrified
Of what you see in the mirror
And where you lost your mind.
Things keep dripping
Right in front of you
You are so empty to care
And so precious to carry.
No one saying thank you
For all you serve and what you made
Yet God sees all.
The harder it rains
The sooner it dies
That's enough to keep trying.
Effort is the key.
Everyone,
Even the ocean
    is born each day.

Prince Siddhartha

Many have known your story
Many have come to tell
The life of Prince Siddhartha
Who gave away his life to free others
From suffering
Who sought another way
Trying everything that was given
And all he had known
Both distances, excess and poverty,
Too much and too little
And finally the middle.

When you were young you walked
From leaf to leaf
Of the lotus bloom
And you were destined for greatness
As a ruler if you wanted
Or as a teacher
So you chose to be.
In finding yourself
You found enlightenment
And showed the way for many.
That was what you were made to do.

As a youth from the kingdom
You had every luxury
And left it all behind
To live in the mind.

You abandoned wife and child
All the plans your father made
To starve yourself and shave your head
And see what life was about
In spite of what the world would say.
Life is suffering and life is pain
We will grow old
And we will grow sick
And one day we all must die
But there's a way to freedom.
Under the Bodhi tree
You saw true peace
And it came by letting go.

Ultimately we find our own path
But we learn through him.
What he achieved.
When we sit down
And hope to find what he found
What's called nirvana

The greatest happiness.
Centuries later
We are with him
We are following what he said
In the way of experience
That folds to the Buddha
It is our nature to be.
Let us be.

ISOLATION

The morning is splendid
Pure as can be
The hour waits for something
I know not yet.
Who waits to arrive
Among the showers of dawn
That fall on sweet silence
That lead me on forgetting
Where it is I started
And what I became.
No more a boy
No more the light of darkness
No more a seed in the sky.
I am less than what I am
More than what I should be
And somehow all these faces are equal
For they are not mine.
Temporary, vacant, somehow strange.
They are more than meets the eye.

In the night air
I feel the wind stir
And touch upon my cheek
Bringing some memory
Of youthful cheer
When so many hopes
Rested on me
And what I would become.
In many ways I achieved
And did what I set out to do.
Many arms were won
Many eyes sought after mine
True hearts were given
And yet a restlessness invaded me
Saying the very life I knew was empty,
Hollow as a shell
For I had given up what I once had
The career I dreamed about
Everything I worked for so long:
For a new city and a chance to really fall in love
With what I have today.
The voice God gave me
And the need to share
How I climbed that mountain

So many years ago
And what it cost me
And what it meant to prove
All the things I said
I knew I could do.
Every sacrifice we took as one.
My mother and father
And the years we spent in solitude
Running as if the whole world depended
Our health and security
Everything I feared since I was a boy.
Now to look back
And see what I gained
For trusting myself
Investing in me
When everyone seemed to say no.
I saw a reflection of myself
When I was young
And how hard I worked back then
How much harder than anyone.
What I gained from that
And what I could be
If only I pushed myself
Invested in me
Dedicated my time to what I believe.
To feel the rising sun
And all it meant to me.

Looking forward to what's ahead of me
To give back to the world
Something good
In the path of freedom.
Laughing.

I had to reach higher
So I would know to go lower.
Everything I thought I needed
I didn't.
Everything I had was too much
So I could be easy on myself
The next time.
Not to say I shouldn't strive
Because the striving was worth it
And a joy in itself.
Just to say I could be happy
With far less.
Whatever I earned
I could give away
And knowing I could do that
Was also worth it.
I had to prove something to myself
And that was enough to turn around
And say I did it.
I had to be sure and certain
I would survive the future years
And give my kids the life
They deserved.
That was happiness too.

I had to reach higher for them
So they would know which way to go
And more importantly
Be free to choose.

Father one day when you go
I'll have everything I need.
The things I built
Was on your foundation.
Everything I spoke
Was with your voice.
And every mistake I made, was mine.
I had to learn that way.
Every time I succeeded
You were there in spirit
Watching me, as I follow you.
Those are big shoes to fill
Bigger now by far.

Lay thee hour down
And let your spirit calm
As of a great peace
The night will come and fix
And bring the form
Of what you desire
Like a spinning wheel
Revolves and turns
We live twice.
Is it who we are
That scares you?
What shape in a foreign sky.
The wrestler throws you down
And your heart is beating
You have fought this battle before
You will stand again.
Disappearing as you always do
As the crowd appears.
They are hungry.
What you grapple
You cannot see.
And you will not submit to this
For they are shadows for you to overcome
All that you have dreamt to be.

Will it matter how you were in the end?
How you were loved and by who?
Name me everything you wanted right now.
How you want to leave the world.
I will say if it's possible
Though I may be wrong
There is some semblance of you in me
And what I would give to see that.
Once I was early and now I'm late
Somehow on time.
There is no reason to give up.
You must go on for me.

The old man proud of his humility
The young child wanting to learn
Never in doubt of their own way.
They are forced to be together
For they have fought each other.
The stares of the old man
Have broken the boy.
He is not as quiet as he appears.
He is full of hatred
For all he assumes
And what he cannot understand.
The boy outshining him
Where he has always tried to compete
He will never admit so
He will never be happy this way
For he is bitter inside
And without love, he has revealed himself
And it is hard to look back.

The swirls of the lake
Give peace by the water
A comfort and protection
Beneath the trees
Sitting on a bench writing
The world inside of me.

What else is there
Of the world outside
That hasn't been sung before?
The children watching
In the late summer
All these things serene
Their voices clutch with the distant birds
For some meaning
Besides seeing.

What settles far away
Are the things we once were
When the future was dim
And there was no end in sight
And I had no place to keep my foot.
Nobody cared as much as me
About my own life.

My heart was heavy
With all the things I might not have again.

A slow recovery
One thing at a time
The leaves, the wind, the earth and sky
Touch upon some victory
Of everything that once was mine.

Now my head aches when I think.
There is a recognition
That something has been done.
It's too painful to celebrate,
And I feel too hurt to cry.

‘So long to so longs
And every so long I’ll think of you’
Those were the words you said.
Was it what you meant?
What falls on snow?
What impurity
Would ever shake that image of you
When you were mine
And you were perfect?
What life outside your head
Outside mine
Would ever compel me
To forget you?
Snow falls
But what falls on snow
What lies, what betrayal
Could ever compare to the agony
Of losing you like this?
Alone I’ve stood for so long
I won’t make it again.
So so long to so longs
And every so long I’ll think of you
If that’s the way
You want it to be.

So full of life I remember
I never laughed that loud before.
When I see you now
I feel the same way
As I did back then.
We were ready for love
And terrified to be in love
And so caught up in love
We missed each other.
We were all nerves back then.

From the dancing mind
Comes a dancing tune,
So turn away your sorrow
And let your feet fly away.
Our love is here forever
Joyous as can be.
Never shall we be alone
For we have each other.
Don't think just feel
The ground beneath your feet
As you slide upon the floor like ice
Gliding the fire
Still burning inside of you.
This is what it is to be young.
I will remember
Forever this day.

THANK YOU

CPSIA information can be obtained
at www.ICGtesting.com
Printed in the USA
BVHW060730090123
655879BV00014B/876

9 798822 908185